THE SLEEP OF FOUR CITIES

THE SLEEP OF FOUR CITIES

Jen Currin

ANVIL PRESS | VANCOUVER | 2005

The Sleep of Four Cities
Copyright © 2005 by Jen Currin

All rights reserved. No part of this book may be reproduced by any means without the prior written permission of the publisher, with the exception of brief passages in reviews. Any request for photocopying or other reprographic copying of any part of this book must be directed in writing to ACCESS: The Canadian Copyright Licensing Agency, One Yonge Street, Suite 1900, Toronto, Ontario, Canada, M5E 1E5.

NATIONAL LIBRARY OF CANADA CATALOGUING IN PUBLICATION DATA

Currin, Jen, 1972-
    The sleep of four cities / Jen Currin.

ISBN 1-895636-70-1

    1. Cities and towns—Poetry. I. Title.

PS8605.U77S54 2005   C811'.6   C2005-905447-6

Printed and bound in Canada
Cover design: Rayola Graphic Design
Typesetting: HeimatHouse

Represented in Canada by the Literary Press Group
Distributed by the University of Toronto Press

The publisher gratefully acknowledges the financial assistance of the B.C. Arts Council, the Canada Council for the Arts, and the Book Publishing Industry Development Program (BPIDP) for their support of our publishing program.

Anvil Press
P.O. Box 3008, Main Post Office
Vancouver, B.C. V6B 3X5 CANADA
www.anvilpress.com

for my beloved siblings

Virginia, Jane, Dan, Cherry, Margaret, Jim, Becky

and for Christine, with deepest love and gratitude

ACKNOWLEDGEMENTS

With deep gratitude for my teachers Beckian Fritz Goldberg and Norman Duble, for their help with these poems.

Thank you to Arizona State University's Creative Writing Program for the graduate fellowship that gave me the time and space to write this book.

Many thanks to my beloved poet-friends for their assistance with these poems and for countless invaluable conversations: Matthew Heil, Charlie Holland, Matt Jolly, Miguel Murphy and Sarah Vap.

Grateful acknowledgement to the editors and readers of the following journals, in which these poems first appeared: *EM Literary*, "The Lesbian Twins," "A Man of Straw," "The Listener in Cap and Bells," "In Search of the Owl's Mirror"; *The Fiddlehead*, "Some Day We Shall Again Live in the Same City," "Atmospheric with Dull Knives"; *River City*, "Two Monologues: The Moon and the Minimalist"; *Washington Square*, "Light of the Land."

TABLE OF CONTENTS

I) MIRROR CITY

A Human Place I Visited Recently While Traveling from Wind to Light	13
The Captain of Love in the Town of Las Lunas	14
Stage Directions for the Stray	16
The Confetti Maker	18
Teeth of the Storm	19
Usages	20
In the City of Limes	21
Shared Dream of the Girl	23
Orange Flowers	24
Light of the Land	26
Loss	28
Three Empty Bottles	29
The "Hundreds of Kisses" Ritual	31
The Lesbian Twins	32
Disembodied Ballad	34

II) EMBRACE OF THE BLUE GARDENS

Plurality	37
The Name That Led the Exiles Out of the Stars	39
The Nudists	41
The Skeleton	42

The Cello Tonguer	44
Sleep	46
A Less Mysterious Source of Lyricism	47
Tempo	49
First Rebels of Spring	50
Birth of the Tide/ On the Crust of Crescent Beach	51
The Mother of All Trees	53
The Green Ones	54
Goodbyes	56
The Knives of Summer	57

III) A TOWN CALLED ORPHAN

A Town Called Orphan	61
In Search of the Owl's Mirror	63
The Listener in Cap and Bells	64
Atmospheric with Dull Knives	66
Exit from a Circular Building	68
Do Not Ring Bells in Her Presence	70
The Touch	72
Botanica: The Penciled Drafts	74
The Snakes of Virginity	76
By the Light of the Midnight Scissors	78
Conversations Set to Music	79
Bald Song	80

IV) A SHELL ON THE BRIDGE

I Swear by the Spiral in the Sky	83
Messages	85
A Man of Straw	87
The Train	89
Subterranean	90
Dear Heaven,	92
A Dance Called the End of the World	93
The Alphabet Backwards	95
The Meditating Androgyne	96
Memoirs of a Shadow	98
I Eat Garlic and the Sun Keeps Them Away	100
Lady Onion, Keeper of the Sorrows	101
Two Monologues: The Moon and the Minimalist	103
Music for Modern Instruments	106
Vertigo	107
A Story in Which the Main Characters are Named Red Bracelets and Night	108
Some Day We Shall Again Live in the Same City	110

MIRROR CITY

A HUMAN PLACE I VISITED RECENTLY WHILE TRAVELING FROM WIND TO LIGHT

When you see your own butcher
scheming in the glow of a bloody lamp—
When the simple life explodes—

You begin to believe the night.

I know it is a perfidious dream,
finite as the summer's lap.
Even as children we waited
to feel the drum's skin.
Life looked difficult
but the sun had somehow made it to the next village
and so would we.

The cheerful knife
held one red hand to the horizon.
We were not the only ones
working nostalgia like a new glove.
The others slept on
stained maps, islands
of salt encrusting their faces.
I could see the death-houses across the rigid ocean,
the glimmering traces of mother's milk—

I got down in the snow
and crawled like a widower
looking for his wife's false eye.
I wanted to be the ice clasping the villagers' hands.
I wanted to be the glass galleon nearing the broken shore.

THE CAPTAIN OF LOVE IN THE TOWN OF LAS LUNAS

Farewell to the violin lessons.
Their heroes were too young to get inside
the lime and salt establishments.
In homage to them,
elders stand out on the sidewalk
begging and borrowing rhythm
from the roses.

The piano player's checkerboard teeth match his songs.
He masters three: *A Bluesman, Not Blind;*
The Dreamland Blues; Blue Sunset Reminiscences.
Wild garden sessions follow
closely behind drugstore buzzes,
games of Follow The Leader.
He always wanted to play the loudest instrument.

His music flies under bridges, over canyons,
so alive only the dead recognize the raw material
of his voice.
He ingests royal meals,
books on tape, various mahogany liquids.
He knows the words to every song in the world.
They come out from between his teeth
ivory-warped, beautifully blackened.

How quickly grandeur crashes,
a flash in the pan
of quick highs, steady lows.
The drumming pervades our dreams,
changes the tempo to *get up and go*.

The wind blows ahead
and gives no details on the ditty.
It has a mind of its own.

STAGE DIRECTIONS FOR THE STRAY

Cough over your shoulder, three days
in shards, making arrangements

for the funeral,
a rush of birds followed
by a spell in bed.

Enter the poem, shabbily dressed.
A girl waiting under the stars.
A wolf crying on the stairs.
A body that wants to be wrung out

like lemons, lemonade smelling
of mud, of rain.

You step one foot into the room.
A packet of salt

tumbles from your pocket.
Enter a man in white.
Enter Pepper, the dark twin.
He wants to take pictures of your feet,
those webs spun overnight
between your toes.

Enter the blue choir in black plastic bags,
soot smeared all over their faces.

They begin to beg
the question as you lose
your voice to static.
The stage darkens. Spotlight
on the plate. One fork, one knife,

one spoon set on the table.

THE CONFETTI MAKER

I would like to be the one on the stairs waving.
The wink of the handkerchief. Let me be
the background music. The bodyguard.
The gravel under your feet.

The hour wears no under or outer garments.
The hour itself is lace, nipple of the clock in love
with sunlight reddening spider's web,
with ants and tall grasses.
A striped snake crosses my path—
what it sheds will be my forever.

I am paper incarnate! Papier-mâché!
I am essential to extravagant parades. Shred me!
From nothingness to newsworthiness,
from down to out—
I am a man fond of throwing things.
In the deepest desert I make snow.

In the future, the present will swivel its hips
to a bastardized version of the past.
It will be my song
shriveling in the flame.
Yes—my echo—for the show of it!—my ballerinas of dust
and light, O temporary stars—

TEETH OF THE STORM

We learn at the Midnight School
that we are nothing.
Talking, we lose our shadows.
The moon carves its light into our door.

The sky is a dream of chase and murder,
of labyrinths and low-growing trees.
Sleep leaves us
for the waking car, the unthinkable
passes through our eyes
where every hero is a flower,
each hour scribbles unforgivable notes:
Car tires screech
like children caught in games.

Every night the corridor and the trains
moaning in memory's ear.
Lightning whitens our eyes,
a purple hue edges the sky.

We watch the dance of unquenchable puppets
through the beaded curtain of rain.
Now a part of the sky is laughing
and in the biblical libraries they are burning
buckets of water.

USAGES

As you sit down to create a love bouquet, go visually.
Remember that it is an idea
hard to justify, a way of making Thursday
a reading from better times.
You can dance to words or eat them.
Maybe you prefer the ending first, like dessert.

Order a gold tooth.
Talk to my good ear.
One thing stands for any other thing.

The nightlife encountered honestly in the urinals
promises no rhyme or reason.
The gargoyle entrusts you with its epiphanies
but not the cutting edge
of the city's prized tool.

Rulers break after repeatedly slapping rebellious hands.
Feet sleep here, people do not.
They make cameo appearances.
They bring their own frames.

IN THE CITY OF LIMES

There is no song that does not sweat here
in the palm of the hand.
Once, I misplaced my key and found a path of bone-stars
which led me to death's childhood
and the lion feeding
on moonless ideas.
He is stone now, no longer stirred
by the golden fans.

The city spreads its watery legs.
Birds break from the trees.
I shake the salt from my rug,
among the wind-garmented
and the pale marbles of my childhood friends.
I open my mouth, a moth
lifts in the breeze.
The incognito hour burns gold.

The trains unload their eggshell sorrows.
Two birds fall from the sky.
I stare into the eye-shaped scab
of the past, ready
to inhabit the shadows
of aprons and dogs.

But the past is not done with me.
It rises from the canal,

licks the lyricism
off the side of my neck,
eclipses the moon,
bleeds a song
stolen from the stone.

SHARED DREAM OF THE GIRL

Hush now, the schoolhouse is in flames.
A sense of you the little rider.
Sleep now, the ocean is at ease.
You are the seal, the rock's insider.

And the words can't make me talk
like the field's cloak of flowers.
She lies faceless in the purple
hinge of the hummingbird's heart.
Her hands have risen to heaven,
they are building a box for her head.
The rest of her body is paint-by-number—
the colour of bottles bobbing in the sweet vinegar sea;
the colour of the seal's eyes; of the ocean, that green bridge.

She did not jump.
Night slipped into her like a fish.
A wall of water cushioned the city.
There was still a trace of blue left in the sky.
She held an egg in one hand and wore wet slippers.
I saw her disperse like ash.

And in the blueberry night you glimmered
like the sudden appearance of a flute among drums.

ORANGE FLOWERS

Do you find it strange
that the designated dreamers
disown their dreams after waking?
They slip into their crumpled second personas
like yesterday's clothes
and step into a day that will not foot/fit the bill,
a night that reaches for the stars
crisp as the smell of rain
in a blackened room.

Distance does not blur. It is all
amazingly clear.
To the locks I talk
but dare not recall the poisoning
of the little ones, the flames and dames,
the long dream.
This song is simply about a goose, a silly goose,
come home to roost,
to cook.

Your matches will not strike anywhere.
They ignite only the automated monster
who slumbers in us all.
I sleep to discover the multiple
dreams of green girls
curling their hair,
sitting on thrones and thorns,

embodying the feminine aspect
more perfectly than the original collector of aprons.

A yellow half-moon
floats in the red rain barrel
like the unanswered question of the day
ushered into this primitive pub crawl
by the governing spirit(s).
Do you not feel
that other verses alluded to this development, this killing
of ill will?

The streets marble with the first drops of rain
as the dream box spills
the slim arms of its finest ingredients.

LIGHT OF THE LAND

My mask hangs by a threat.
I part the curtains, quote
my ignorance.
The hours fan themselves.
One by one, I see them drop.

I didn't know I was stealing.
I thought I was just making music
while the mice
ran up and down the stairs.

The parking lot lit up like a stage,
milk of applause
accompanied by a hobo wind
pulling me homeward . . .

🍂

Such cold coats, the cots.
Like a moth's death in a monk's cell.
Pull the wool over my eyes, I will
be the prize bullfighter,
see the rust of the world darken to plum
as the sea air steps
from my lungs.

❦

A taxi tempts me. I have no change
in my pockets or my embroidered purse.
I would like to encounter
the potent agent of dawn
in the space between the violin
and its bow.
I pull off a few eyelashes.

❦

Telephones ring in my ears
as I swim.
My bald cousins, the sand dunes, echo
the sea's every word.
Soon I will be sipping from the cat's bowl.

LOSS

    A long hour, a thread,
    dark hair in your soup, the tea
    silent and strong,
    each speaker as if
    already dead
    walking in circles as the grass grows
    to cover the globe
    in death-water, where we watch
    our blackest reflection, this story
    that could be anyone's.

I don't remember
the belt buckle, just the cowboy hat
and boots, cat dismembering cat,
a shrill voice at the next table, a film still
where the buttons melted.
We sip our common sleep.
The birds panting, their beaks open—

I hand you a gold pen, your signature
splashes, a fountain.

I have an inkling you'll tell me on the elevator.
You and I—we'll wring the laughter
out of this
as the rescuers lift us like violins.

THREE EMPTY BOTTLES

I was resting in the nausea shed,
humming the neatness of February,
thinking of the dictionary in suite five,
its *never, never.*

One fish left, another came to join me.
We shared irregular odes,
insomniacs in spirit.
It was many hours before we blew out the candles.

❧

Loan me the night,
tell the easy stories
of coin fountains in a drink-shop
where my persona
slowly carves his sonnet
out of soap and water.

When he calls to the words,
a sugar bowl spills
its silence on the floor.

❧

Home knows how far
the door is, it opens

like a book
to the knocking of the waves.
This flower is my next of kin,
it belongs to the camera, memory's
dumb trespasser.

❦

In the deep slums of ocean,
we balance slim emotions
on the blades of our tongues.
We plant the dead
with herbs and dry words.
In costume jewelry, mute as paper cuts,
we take the bath with language.

THE "HUNDREDS OF KISSES" RITUAL

Have you heard of the gold man,
the silver man selling
his pleasure message?
The priestess who requires two bodies
for the image, one light and one dark?

A shadow in her goblet;
throw down the gauntlet
and the forest takes the clearing hostage.
Where once struggle had no place . . .

First, cut out their tongues.
The last drop heralds the first incantation
as damp faces tamp the infant's intuition
with stony and harsh rhymes,
a certain mixture of privacy and openness.

In earshot of the moon (a tambourine),
in the airborne taste of tangerines,
in lieu of three thousand suicides,
one sight:

a black figure croons, leans over the crib.

THE LESBIAN TWINS

Breast
You are the one I will take for my bride.
No—you are the girl to dry my feet
with your hair. My name is Breast.
I will honor you under the table
at breakfast.

Ankle
I am struck by the number of clocks
in your house. I turn
over a new sheet
and you are sleeping in my bed again.

If I awake to unawareness,
my parrot's wooden cousins
will give up speech
for a transparent dwelling.

Breast
And she will throw stones
if you give her a glass of water.
You'll need a candle and a mirror,
something to colour
your hair. As the shadows
press a spider into the wall,
remember the gateway of your skin.

Ankle
Like a bull I continue to break pitchers,
to assure another tragedy
shall not visit my family.
Death might appear as a bald woman
with impossibly large earrings.
She will tell us: *Nothing is burning.*
It just smells that way.

Breast
In a school without windows,
I buy my puppets.
They will be my kindling when I break
to picnic with the stars.

DISEMBODIED BALLAD

So we have entered and re-entered
this confusion, contraption of monsters,
this thick, state-of-the-art
time. Darkness coats
each of us, we carry
snapshots of infants and leaves.
Only the flowers sigh,
fully giving up sympathy.

Someone else wears the necessary uniform,
knows the imbrication of selves.
We are but petals, ten fingers,
two hands, a circle of sticks and stones.
We are a thorn of midnight at the end of a golden tunnel.

And the stars—they are islands.
There is more to them
than meets the eye.
If it is not too much of a leap,
we must lift them down carefully
like the small pieces of summer
here on loan.
When we boil down the bones,
words occur,
the night releases its white fish
and we that are left—

EMBRACE OF THE BLUE GARDENS

PLURALITY

Peek through the holes in the wooden door.
Now you see her sleeping
on her bramble bed, lit like a torch
from her toes to her head
propped up by ruins.

Centuries later, you steal her grave goods.
No one, no thing
watches you.
Your affairs of sugar and water
dissolve into speeches,
closet confessions
of one who has the grace to relinquish her accent,
who recognizes this is not, nor will it ever be,
a movie.

If only you had been an ordinary woman,
but the harmony maneuvers, tunnel struggles
and masquerades reveal
there is no ordinary.

☙

I do not repent.
I love greatly until I'm spent
and day tosses our peasant names out the window
of a yellow farmhouse bordered by a mint green field.

The rooster crows *not one dawn, many.*
Two sisters make vests
out of newspaper.

When they decide to participate, they cancel their subscriptions
and call this sleep *Revolution*.
They write letters to the grave which unites us.

THE NAME THAT LED THE EXILES
OUT OF THE STARS

These tourists will endure
torture. It is worth it
every time we kiss
through a barricade of lisping soldiers.
So you were a vagabond bound
for Vegas on a northern train.
So I was the ugliest little boy
walking on clouds.
I take off my shirt, you light me.
Can we crab walk up the mountain?

Waking on the beach,
an overcoat for a blanket—
my toes are cold as the fire
has gone out.
A snow of ash and newspaper,
violence of the red apartment,
the viper's newest alphabet
we cannot read.

I always knew our twenty-year marriage
wouldn't last the night.
Still it is so nice to roll over
onto you in the morning.
Can I take you down
to the river which is wearing

its floral dress?
It might be spring
weighing lightly on our shoulders.
It might be the world
in our small kitchen,
burning down the worm of its wick.

THE NUDISTS

On Tuesday she blissed the hours with open-mouthed kisses.
The sun crawled through the window
on its hands and knees, its juices
ran down her chin. I eased off the dragon robe,
the room levitated,
we found ourselves embracing over the sea.

Now she is the sob of a train.
In bed I lay, begging for her back
to be turned to me.
I write letter after letter on moon stationery: *O my*
forest, my pineapple, my sandal,
my thread . . .

If only someone would throw a rock at the streetlight,
but now the firewomen arrive to shine their trucks,
the station lets out a scream

and the blue is quite blue, my love, the green—

THE SKELETON

The sun is an onion.
I see glass, green in your eyes.
Let the wind be your pick-me-up,
for the chimes are not death rattles.

Words fall over one another
like dominoes, tattletales
who steal toes from the frozen.
The moon proposes marriage,
strikes a bargain:
a ceremonial necklace for an unlucky coin.
The beaded babe boils water
for coffee and steps
to the corner store for milk and honey.

Frame the hour, sweet and sour, drawn to scale.
First a tangerine, now a margarita.
Clothes used or new to see through
a bottle of tequila, airplane size.
Mittens to keep the mystery warm,
like breath.

The skeleton loves his boxing gloves.
He breaks the curse of water
when he comes home alive
with pockets full of golden hair.

Like a mouth to flame
I love you. I love
the sound of trains.
Here is an apple and some ice water.
Take the music
and follow its misdirections. The bells
ring singly with the solitude
of an umbrella indoors.

THE CELLO TONGUER

Torn from the notebook of creation,
my feelings will never change.
In other worlds, words, and works
in wax, perhaps, but not here
in the river adjacent to the volcano
where a bald girl washes her only dress
and the crescendo is just
the beginning.

Her fine timing unearths the bottle opener
and the tuning in the brewery.
A high tide swallows the beach
for the first time in one hundred years.

This girl is not made of stone.
She boards a train to buy eggs.
She rides shotgun in the owl hour,
dark behind her ears, anticipating
a shadowed bend in the road.

In towns called Jewel and Mist,
in drifts of fog
produced by the mattress factory,
in a green paper crown,
she drops no hints, is lit
by the light of the fish tank,
warps the harps of winter,
warms her hands.

She draws the curtains
and fills the room.

—*for Sorrell*

SLEEP

We'll scale the hours like cathedrals
or castles inhabited by the makers of myth,
forced into these roles
as if they were wooden shoes
and now the dancing, the drooling,
the birthing on the balcony.

Compose a hymn for those very dead.
This is no day to be out of doors.
A sleight of the snow-artist's hand
smudges the garden.
The sleigh waits.
We cannot ask for more than the tapping
of our feet as the windmill spins
slow songs.

In the tiger-blink of an eye,
crows fly
out the window,
the clocks seated around the dinner table
resume their chiming.
From the land of lost laughter,
a lonely assassin stumbles.

A LESS MYSTERIOUS SOURCE OF LYRICISM

I abandon my rooftop view,
creep through the mouse hole
into the hollowed-out dream of a hailstorm.
The throbbing skyline
forges hindsight, *What circumstance*
will you wear this evening?

Long day until the stone tower collapses,
I hang a skin on the line.
It's been a tent for many, a refuge
from the grassy rain and "take a leaf" thieves
who say goodbye
but never manage to leave.

≋

Trace a shadow on the wall in watercolour
as the clay light dwindles.
We too are in need of fine materials, brave
and abrupt laughter,
guns and diamonds, daughters
in motion.

Six tattoos among us, we rebuff
the chief chemical:
Study our handwriting,
hind wing of star bird.

*Into the scripted sack for sleeping,
this little-known throat clearing
believes in revision of the spoken word.*

TEMPO

Whether or not they belong to us, these buildings
are our children. They salute the lavender sky.
Humbled, we burrow in the neighbouring field
as the limping well-wishers place victory wreaths
on the rooftops.

We had wondered if they would treat
us like a real town
but after several races they ceased to cheer us on.
We never watched yesterday. We forgot to wash
the long ears, the shadow dancers
of all shapes and sizes
who tucked candles in their turbans.
The piano poured a mahogany tune in our ears
as the room lapsed subterranean.

I only know the breast stroke
and perhaps that's no longer enough.
May I make a call, one call?
Will you share my tea water,
never shave,
learn to walk slowly,
lisp a love of place?

Beat of a drugged drummer,
can you shrug to this?

FIRST REBELS OF SPRING

In torn skirts on the outskirts of the city
we wait for daybreak, for the troupe of musicians and dancers
in their orange tunics,
for the fire to revive us
so we may compose wet odes
under the blue unconcern of new sky.

Music floods the road.
Never anything to live for
but this: brambles, marble sounds
of rain melting a house
in which participants converse
in equally unbelievable tones.

The chairs fly around the room
as my lover slices
a pineapple. She chews gum
while playing the guitar. Many students
practice here because of the location.
Nothing private, nothing new
as messengers cart bundles of words
from the temple to the river.

I traded my spirit for a handful of nails.
Bliss pinched my elbows.
The stars climbed back up on the roof
and the sky said *hurt me.*

BIRTH OF THE TIDE/ON THE CRUST OF CRESCENT BEACH

The shadow of my youngest sister opens a door in the sand
as she flies parallel to the shoreline,
horizontally at home
as a sea or sand crab.

I'm climbing out of a tidal pool,
testing my unwebbed toes
for the first time.

We are to meet at the union
of the river and the sea.
We are to dance in the wedding party,
to offer a splash of music
with a flute, a fiddle, a few drumsticks.

She lands on the beach
singing of broomsticks.
Now I am a horse and I offer her a ride.

Somewhere among the forest's foxgloves and ferns
an orange-bellied salamander
slows the green hours of celebration.
The baby floats down the river
laughing, clapping his hands.

My sister carries the moon in her basket.
We have the sun on our side.
When the child arrives we will feast
on night, desert day.
We will dip in our skins,
swoop up like birdwomen
as the baby tears rhythm from clay.

—for Virginia

THE MOTHER OF ALL TREES

Over the endangered species, through the dappled forest, up Smoke Mountain and halfway down the other side, you will find a cabin tucked under the largest spruce tree.

The two rooms smell of lavender and indecision, the air is weighted with the ESP of organic house plants. Flirtations of saxophone and flute float down from the loft, mingle with candle shadows on the walls and floor. The song is spacious, evocative of gift baskets.

Sap coats your hands and arms, your clothing. You unlatch your guitar case. A velvet heart beats softly inside.

To have come so far
to where the leaves themselves are flowers.

Four paces to the sparrow's window
where the sea opens its gallery of breath and breadth—
The true length of a line—
The human condition—
Its oils, its vinegars—

THE GREEN ONES

Powder drama of the worms, two dogs
in mud masks prance under a silver sun
where purple bells and river stench
break the day's routine.
Old women carry young trees
up to the balcony,
one root in the grave.

They swallow the new moon's instructions
with a pinch of salt.
We are all in the dark.
Who saves us? The spade
and the dedicated orphans
who write books and unite seas.

Light flings a handful of stars into the foggy morning.
Shadow is a tightrope walker
balancing the world on its forehead
and the elephant is improbable,
a landscape unto itself.

Walking across the desert in boatman pants and mossy wigs,
the women contrive
to finance the dance
with snake eyes, a green marble,
a circle-shaped deck of tarot.

First card: *The garden confesses, "I ate the fountain.
She was a handsome devil, compelling
as a well-told lie."*

                                    Second: *The longest dog climbs
into a snowdrift, sleeps
and awakes half-human.*

Third: *Dealing seeds for the hunger,
the sunflower heals the sun.*

GOODBYES

The saxophone left a hole in the song
when it slipped from the house.
Now the rooms can hold no echoes. The rain
relays its message on the roof:
The animals, the animals
are arriving.

The lit cigar of the moon
drops its shadowy ashes,
night shakes the lice from its fur.
Rumors of a song hitchhiking
down the coast, hungry
and alone in a lonely landscape,
ten eyes in its feet, two eyes in its head,
drinking the red wine of exhaustion.

The rain sings in melodious tongues,
faces drawn in the window's fog.
The guitar breathes in a forest of ghost trees
sliced by bird whistle, human whistle.

Outside the house, calla lilies
release the two-headed voice.
It leaps when spoken to, it speaks
in the somber, the stoic, the laughing, the longing, the calm.

THE KNIVES OF SUMMER

There are flowers of royalty, enormously angelic.
They sing and my garden only hears about it.
There is love and there are lovers.

In the amber loneliness of late afternoon,
I sing and the forest swells its blood symphony—
leaves through light on their way to the river,
wind spiriting the green bottles of trees.

In another existence we lived in the drum as one.
Clouds crushed winter quietly.
A knocking woke us: *Come down off the mountain!*
The end is in bloom!

Under the closed eye of the half-moon,
foaming nightdresses rise and fall,
the ivory lighthouses blink.
One thousand islands and not one dream
growing greener.

The season knots and bites its thread.
It speaks in the sharp dialect of birds.
Once we lived in the full moon of a drum.
A shadow passed over the sea.
Curious bird, memory

A TOWN CALLED ORPHAN

A TOWN CALLED ORPHAN

This summer invite the rapist
to run away with you. She is so pretty

when she smiles. Those long fingers
stretching silences, sentences

standing on their toes.
In an orange dress, red bracelets,

you kiss the toad.
All the hells swirl around your ankles,

the treasure hut collapses.
Weren't you two giggling in the forest

like leaves?
How very early of you

to hang the moon
on the remaining wall.

Now you both fall to the floor,
claiming sleep drank you

through a net of holes.
Now I can blink

and grow my white beard.
The sky swells with your absence—no balloons.

Who can read to a child
these words?

IN SEARCH OF THE OWL'S MIRROR

So it happens I am mortal: my heart,
a cluster of fruit flies, whirrs
in the heat of my chest.

I bequeath my chair and birdcage
to a girl who plays
the violin. I leave one match
in a book of matches on my desk.
Near a river, I encounter night.

Sometimes the milk we drink
turns black in our mouths.
The baby I picked up yesterday
is now a vial of dirt
from my hometown.
Sometimes we're forced to don clothes
made of chance.

I awake in a field, wearing
a stranger's shoes.
Is the night as forgetful as I am?

The moon has left its half-eaten dish in the sky,
the wind scatters the past
like bread crumbs.
I'm hungry.

THE LISTENER IN CAP AND BELLS

The bloody pen records a dream
of your death, a wet dream
of ocean, a dry dream of cemeteries
at the city's edge.

(I write this in parenthesis
because I'm dead.)

Yesterday I was a wheel,
chilled by the sight of children
playing as the day laid down
its hat and we asked one another
to act like human beings.

Spokes of laughter carved my throat.
I harboured a hatred for birds,
the pale blossoms
they left on my coat.
I don't mean to ridicule them,
but what they know of suffering
could fill a thimble.

Every time I look up, the white buildings
close their blue sky eyes,
a cloud crosses the window
of my mind, and I'm certain I am sleeping.
Only there

could I be this broken—
picking up pieces of myself and looking at them,
bewildered.

ATMOSPHERIC WITH DULL KNIVES

In the shout lounge I tasted my first beverage,
bitter as the green thorns embroidered
on the barstool's cushion. The music
sounded like crickets. My toes
were one by one getting it wrong,
stepping into the lies
with their listening.

It was like birth, the shedding
of silence, a long corridor
followed by so many troublesome
hands. Stitched together with weak thread,
sent out to sea with only
the hope of drowning.

I spent the rest of the night
spilling drinks on my companion.
Later, I studied the underside of a table.
I wanted to remain invisible at all costs,
but my hiccups gave me away.

༄

Yesterday on the pier I saw a ship
with five sails. I saw another with none.
I turned back to my book.
When I looked up, the sail-less ship

had blossomed—two handsome triangles fluttered,
white as nursery bed sheets.

And as I sat there, the wind read the book
rapidly, with no regard for rhyme.

EXIT FROM A CIRCULAR BUILDING

A burst of light at the door—
The moon drops its ladle
like the brightest
of blindfolded angels.
I fold up my portable altar.

At the station, you kiss
strings of pearls,
pull rings from your bag
and put them on—
You do not miss me.

I don't know why the wind carries
no grudge.
In the hall of rubbish and waste
I am filled with ingratitude.
I dream of slicing the king cake, finding
the time when the front of the room
became the back of your hand.

I wanted to dance
with you because you didn't
know how. I held out my arms
ribboned with scars.
A thread glinted between us.

And now—every time you move,
a package arrives in your name.
Butter melts on the stove.
The day creaks open.
I sweep up yesterday's words.

DO NOT RING BELLS IN HER PRESENCE

A strand of hair holds my place
in the book which rattles
like glass in a bag.
I know my audience: she is
the slip of paper
that came with my birth-purchase.
She is the one
I cut myself on,
descending the stairs
of her sigh. Her eyes close
their gates.
I am back at the game that hurts me.

Last night I couldn't see
what kept me from my own gray hands,
the buildings floating outside my window.
I drank for the shine it gave me,
the sound of two inches
sloshing in a glass.

Should you plan to visit her: bring boyish clothes,
a proud tilt to your chin.
Empty your pockets
and give her the key
to the heart of your apartment.

Reborn as a pen, she plans
to alter the names
in my account. I let her.
She leaves her panties on the chair
when she goes.

THE TOUCH

I want to hear the slap
of your shadow
as it hits the floor,
the pins and needles
of water falling
tap to tub. I'm tired,
and what you know
about me will soon be written
on a postcard and passed
in the night.

We're down to the last few bites.
Those who are in the habit
of eating parsley off their plates
will not help us.
Wine has cast its blood-shadow
across our cheeks.

I've come in off the street
to confess these crimes.
We have several mothers in common,
and while they plot our deaths
I want to give them something
to talk about.

I've misspelled my own name so many times
and still I remember every syllable

of every spell.
Still I remember you humming
along as the ghosts
drank water in the kitchen,
as our mothers counted our fingers and toes.

BOTANICA: THE PENCILED DRAFTS

On the battlefield I buttered bread, whistling
as the sun broke its promise.
An egg landed in my lap.
I had to cross the table to help myself.
I made alliances. The ants
wore me and I wore
red sandals. I carved
a tree stump with our initials.

All was calm, until I noticed
the slippery fins of the flower bucking
just beyond my reach.
My reverie ground to a halt
with a dinner fork grimace.

I found what I thought to be night,
a black billboard
propped up by static.
Here I had been courting the petals of silence,
praising the motives of pencils—
as if I had hands!
The sky fidgeting above me
for years as I read
to butterflies, knowing
I'd never see straight again—

I envied the shy fish
their miniature castles;
the serpent, its fan.
I wanted my tongue to split
on the bridge
so that I could spit without rehearsal.
Of course you know all of this
is now irreversible.

THE SNAKES OF VIRGINITY

Outside the window, the river tastes
of apples. You swam there, secure in the school
of your fish tattoos,
comforted by birds who used the leaves
to see, low birds
stung by bells.

You said: *Merely looking at land*
or sea will turn one eye lazy
and give the mind over to knocking.
I sat there clad in flies.
I didn't know any better.
My people had cautioned me it was for the best.

And yet there was a notable absence
of lyricism in your speech when you told me
your one thought was to feel
his throat in your hands.
The small lizard continued to give you
dry kisses all the way up your arm.

Sometimes we slept in the woods
in men's trousers. We were merciless
when it came to the urgings
of our bones—burning our bodies
at both ends.

From your lips grew a long vine.
I climbed it and came to a gathering
that could have been a wedding or funeral—
the guests wore both black
and white. They mingled aboard
a sternwheeler. I swam
in the froth of their wake, my head
just above water, water
in my eyes
as when I first held
your choker of garlic.

BY THE LIGHT OF THE MIDNIGHT SCISSORS

In the wee hours I was led by the hand
down a block of lemonade stands,
seduced by the bartender's stubble and the image
of your hem sweeping the wet asphalt.

Words were lost in the conversation's rubble
as you shredded newspaper for an impromptu campfire.
A foghorn liberated me
from the need to reply.
You knew all my letters
were photocopied from books
I took out of the library,
and I knew I could no longer wear
the wig you made for me
out of my own hair.

CONVERSATIONS SET TO MUSIC

Foot in my mouth, I swear
I never set foot in her house. Where she sleeps
I slept. But every lock
was out of key.
There were certain blue curtains
that I never understood.
I could not stand on my head
to please her.

Each night a mouse under the table
enjoyed the crumbs of our labours.
I stuttered through meals,
counting every hair on its head.
Her stomach for spirits
and spiritual connection with cigarettes
brought a teary taste to my cup,
but I had to drink the tea to read the leaves.

We learned to sew
at one another's knees.
All our lies
fit tidily into two trunks.
That last day I stole the neighbour's shutters
from right under her nose.
She didn't smell it coming—

I was the swift guest, that gust
of wind.

BALD SONG

If she outwears me, I'll live on
in this old man's skin
of a pinstriped suit.
I hope not to forget her,
for I've been known to lose people
over the summer,
just as, at times, an umbrella turns into a glass of water
in my hand.

A SHELL ON THE BRIDGE

I SWEAR BY THE SPIRAL IN THE SKY

I was born in the well. Night arrived
in the form of a candle. I swallowed
the stars along with my mother.
An ache in my knees spelled travel
as I climbed the ladder,
shedding my body's hair.

My first opera: the hysterical
sobbing of hunting dogs, a deer
swimming in the river.
I wound bandages around my head.
I didn't want to see this.
But what came next I was born to endure:

Swirl of the frightened waters,
my boots sunk in the bank,
a dead fish in my palm
like the foulest of prayers.

༄

I'm a sop for narrative.
Give me a hand, I'll squeeze,
but it takes the zest of eighteen limes
to seduce my tongue into licking the plate,
my fingers into curling a fist
tight as the onion's bulb.

That's how you'll find me, at mid-morning,
sorting the darkest chocolates
in the depths of the cellar's yawn.
You'll ask me why I no longer coo
with the clouds. And I'll tell you
of the sweetest branch held out to me
when I was drowning . . .

—for Jane

MESSAGES

I do not know how long the trance lasted.
I cannot describe the world in boxes like time.
I might have died
and swum through the underwater caves
of a dazzling dreamstate.
I might have killed.
It's like reaching your hand
into a bag of hands
and coming out empty-handed.

Great audiences invent audible ceilings.
A few boys attend these performances
and bring palm branches for the fanning.
Some songs cave in toward the end.

Dark singing
causes the audience to laugh and lean forward
into the next spring.
The conductor dares to detach the melon moon.
All musical notes drift coastward
to the place where the scripts have bitten
off more than they can chew
and walk miles and miles
in no one's shoes.

It might be interesting
to hear the ending think out loud:

I've seen students spit upon reason
as the source of mediocrity.
I've redeemed the shattered windows
of a lyrical city.
As for all of you, you'll have to patch together
a new eyesight.
Take a plane somewhere. Do not land.
Tell your friends
who wanted to be invited
that they can't come.
Tell the dead
they've been forgotten.

A MAN OF STRAW

Once a redheaded boy in a city park
wrote me this poem:
*Your eyes are the twelve colours
of my beard.*

I kept the poem for years in my wallet,
pulling it out at parties
to impress new acquaintances.
It was the one possession that defined me.

Years ago, you gave me a striped sweater.
Or perhaps it was solid—some fictitious colour
we attribute to the ocean
when we cry.
I strangled the sweater
just for the fun of it.
I was that sick.

And then there was the joke
about the ugly bride,
unveiled for your father
on special occasions.
He laughed with the rest of us
until he disappeared.
We found him later, floating
in the green pond,
his long hair wound
into the shape of a life preserver.

Even now, when I glance at your wrist, I see it.
I take it close to my face,
I read it like a psalm.

THE TRAIN

Look sleepless, spider of time.
Keep away from children.
Read the sign language of doors.
Let the traveler wake
the clocks as doves
crumb the bread.
Just now, three friends are tuning the piano
with their laughter.

Drink quickly, the kiss deepens
to green river.
Yes her eyes are fish.
In them, your scent goes blind
as a bonfire near the river's edge.
In them, the winter painter tastes icicles
as his portrait melts.

You exit the forest of milk-sweating trees.
Horses and roses loom in your ruby windows.
Silver crutches gleam in the fields.
Shrug off sleep, spider. A tuxedo darkens
in the last car.
Don't turn your back
on the sky. The pink
will not hold.

SUBTERRANEAN

In the nearly edible light
I brush off your wig.
From death, you blush.

The claws holding up the tub
crawl across the floor
as the snow quickens.
Pieces of your hair fall into the wastebasket.
I step into the bath with your best friend.

You sip coffee in a crumbling villa
as night sets its glittering watches
on your cheeks. Your mother's perfume
walks the tattooed halls.
On the beach, children throw rocks
at seagulls.

The piano sings from the house
of your mouth.
You have sat in both of our chairs
and now recite the insinuations
of the maritime libraries.

Your friend washes her nipple rings
as I lift the water jar
from the windowsill.
Outside the snow is spinning sugar tales.

And I've spent the dark pennies of blood
gathered from your bedroom floor.
My tongue tells her body to weep.
I miss your inked sleeves.

DEAR HEAVEN,

On First Street I saw you clapping.
I could sing you a song about girls
dancing on a bridge.
I caught a chant on the sled ride
down, but the me of yesterday
is no longer relevant
so thank you for your rhyme.

During that seamless time you lived as a snake
hellbent on swallowing its own tail.
You did not dirty your mind with the past
and would not let the world take you.

We have separate beds in our dreams
where we encounter different and indifferent
words from childhood.
Go deeper into one self, you will never lose the one
or the many—
your violinist playing for the gold gypsy,
the boy on the blue pier.

Always in spring
this uprising.
You let go of the string and look back over your shoulder.
Can't you see me waving
in the wings of blue-black birds?
Do you know how far we are from language?

—for Cherry

A DANCE CALLED THE END OF THE WORLD

Pack up your seven plums, the bruise
of your eye shadow as you turn
on your heel.

Which dance is this?
Not the one where he lifts you
over his head, saying,
You'll never be this.

Nor the one where you clench
the plastic stem between your teeth,
walk the tightrope across the street
to another house where she climbs
from her box and taps
you on the shoulder,
spins you to the window—

The conversations—now those were dances—
punctuated by bright fliers
advertising the shark in your basket,
still frozen after all your travels.

Up ahead, the ghosts are already boarding the train.
This dance will be a swift one: You woo her
by bringing a ladder to her balcony,
a portable radio. Her last letters crackle
in your back pocket.

You think it ought to be raining
but it is summer at the time
and the threats from the street can't reach you.

THE ALPHABET BACKWARDS

This is for the apple poet, the poet of insomnia,
the never-potted poet
may his feet break soil.

This is for the dream we both remember.

Can you sleep? Count the sheep. Be the black one
falling down the aisle of forgetfulness,
climbing up the steep cliff
into the armpit of the abyss.
Go beyond brevity. Smell that hound.
Grasp the collar and stop breathing,
start feeding off the lines of the lion,
the depths of the tiger
performing leaps, perversions
hot under the jowls, your back to the stall
of the underworld.

You wrote in smoky script:
*I've been lifted
and my hooves again touch the ground . . .*

I went there to find you and I found
you holding the girl-poet's blonde hand.
You ran your fingers through the air,
present as the fantastic sound of the sea
in the rooms of an empty farmhouse in Iowa
where I owe you, heart of a feather—

—for Dan

THE MEDITATING ANDROGYNE

I sleep with witches.
Days of dishes ushering
the dust into my bed—
They hang orange lanterns in my room.

Lighthouses of their eyes.
Night in the middle of the day.
I pass them eating lunch on the benches,
wine jars filling with rain.
My heart competes with the birds.

Death is the newborn
of hermits
in the hills above the city.
Sipping from their shoes,
pregnant women
see faces in the leaves.

Throat bells.
I've come to tell you how much the trees,
the worms—saying *today*—
playing tomorrow
on an island of children
where one can still
wash a shirt in the sea.

I will always wonder
who paid the piper,
who cut the eyes
of mold from the bread.
Will I die dancing?
Will I die
standing on my head?

MEMOIRS OF A SHADOW

Black wind woke me
shortly before midnight.
Dried blood flickered on the walls.

Deep into the segregated jungle
I sought this secrecy
like the tarot cards of a lover's eyes.
Monkeys chattered overhead.
Occasionally, I caught sight of a mud-streaked girl
hiding behind turquoise leaves,
calling out rain messages to the birds.

We saw the moon's fingerprint
on the graves of stones.
Fragrant grasses fed our hungers.
There were paper blossoms that smelled
of schoolroom glue, words
I could not recognize
etched into fallen trees.
At times, the heavy silence seemed to await
a spark, but I did not speak,
for I feared fire
and we had not yet found the mossy river.

The girl gurgled like the daughter
of a waterfall. Many-melodied
birds trembled in the trees.

It would take us a long time
to know one another.
It would take us to the fishes
walking on paths of spilled darkness,
to the cups overturned,
the cups overflowing.

I EAT GARLIC AND THE SUN KEEPS THEM AWAY

If the prescription is for thorns,
call the doctor who hours her days
with anecdotes of animals
who were once women.
She turned my sister into a crow.
My lover became a horse.
Who will be the bear
she puts in the sky
and tells to stay there?

In these hissing ruins, we hear the forest
whisper its incest.
Teased by the acrobats
in miserable states of undress,
you find the peacock's inner child.

She's handing you real butter, my friend,
not margarine. Make a note in the margin:

*I searched the house,
I could not find your keys.*

LADY ONION, KEEPER OF THE SORROWS

In a green temple at the bottom of the sea
I wear a bracelet given to me by the garbage can.
Which hand holds the red feather,
which the dove?

A bone washed up on the beach
couldn't have put it better.
These eyes all see me horizontally, like the bananas
hung over the door.
In the shadows a woman
fans herself with a bouquet.
It's such a fragrant day, I start to say to her,

but she has ears only
for the shell that bellows
like a crushed bug.
The tea is licorice and laced
with the scent of campfires.
A candle flickers in my cup.
Like a kiss, the burn
won't stop burning—
Even now the forest gnaws its blue flutes,
the drummers drink their own urine.

She wrings the onion juice from her handkerchief
Now she weeps, now that our woes
have subsided. Stitches arch

where her eyebrows once were,
her mouth is a hole punched in the sky.

TWO MONOLOGUES: THE MOON AND THE MINIMALIST

Moon
In the spirit of friendly vandalism,
I fed them legends of rain.

Minimalist
The chair I sat on caused no discomfort.
It was the only one in the room.

Moon
So I said, you may piss on the tracks,
but you must realize—I see you.

Minimalist
There was only a slice of light.
I often left the door ajar.

Moon
Two girls soothed their feet
with olive oil. This pleased me.

Minimalist
I drank tea without lemon.
I shook my laundry out on the bed.

Moon
The drunk ghosts always carouse
during this blind month of December.

Minimalist
Lights, darks—I was at a loss
for socks. I made an entry
in my albino diary.

Moon
At such times, I watch only black and white movies.
I vacate the moment when necessary.

Minimalist
I saw it through a thin curtain
of hair: girls throwing tangerines at the new boy.

Moon
I can be as starry-eyed as the constellations,
as jubilant as the train's horn.

Minimalist
A boy with cigarette burns on his arms.

Moon
I had an errand—
a pair of earrings to return.

Minimalist
Just this morning,
I broke my fast
with a piece of toast.

Moon
Just this morning,
I halved the whole.

MUSIC FOR MODERN INSTRUMENTS

The birds are in the violin
music, habit-forming house
of cupboards stocked with Big Dipper, Little Dipper, North Star.

I lived on the sound for ten days
and spent another seven supping on the smell
so now it does not matter
if I develop an oral fixation or lease
my lover's menstruation shack:
I'm all the gladder,
welcoming the warm tide,
true to the tenor of a day
that forgets to be faithful
to any one person or idea.

Now an athlete of the third tier
types up her secrets:
He painted horses.
I saw the book cover.
No water or electricity
for two weeks! Such a halo!

In six or perhaps nine months
I will return to the neighbourhood
and I expect to find everything the same:

Burning oriency of dawn,
impossible city where no city should be.

VERTIGO

A system of grunts and hisses,
scratch at the window, shell
in the ear, one eye
to the sunrise shuddering
behind a palm tree.

What language really does for us—
to ease the ailment—drops
in the abyss bucket.
Strike a match against the cave wall
and blink, fall.

Wisemen in robes of spray paint
crawl down the dusty road. Sunset hits
but we have already seen enough: Mouths of trees
unlocked by countryside wails, emotions
of a red moon.

In the animal glow of a fidelity lullaby,
we dig a tunnel
for the characters who climb out of the spine.
We leave the book to eat its own pages.

A STORY IN WHICH THE MAIN CHARACTERS ARE NAMED RED BRACELETS AND NIGHT

It takes place in the sea forests,
where a bar of soap can turn
into a bass guitar, into a woman
singing bitter lyrics. Who can blame her?
She is shut tight in a jar.

It is similar to the old tale of seals
shedding their skins, resuming
their human lives for one day
of the year.

Night contrives to have others
take care of him.
He gets them to feed his birds.
So dark in the sea forest,
when Red Bracelets leaves, there is no one
to look after the children.
They forget to comb their hair,
they run wild, they eat weeds.
They do not open
her cabinets, or touch
the green dust.

Books were Red Bracelets' bedfellows,
and now that she is gone—

The characters lie to themselves,
they lie down and the foxes come
to steal their faces.

—with thanks to Matt Jolly

SOME DAY WE SHALL AGAIN LIVE IN THE SAME CITY

Mother plays the flute and she's mad.
Her sentences need stilts.
Her paintings never dry.
Her clocks say, *Come in, I'm open.*
Later, they are institutionalized.

A selection of round and fancy eyes
fills the suitcase. Fog mystifies the front door's glass.
Outside: an unsettled debt, a fingernail moon.

The stoic weeps not.
All the sharers of her experience
lower their voices
and prepare for the next storm watch
with a candle, a seafarer's song,
a match.

I can see the dawn
lit like a patient lamp
on the other side of night's door.
I step out onto the porch.

Better the light than I—
searching the wet streets for the first ocean.

ABOUT THE AUTHOR

Born and raised in Portland, Oregon, Jen Currin currently lives in Vancouver, B.C. with her wife, Christine Leclerc. She is a member of the poetry collective *vertigo west*.

OTHER ANVIL PRESS POETRY TITLES

Bizarre Winery Tragedy / Neff / $14
Bogman's Music / Armstrong / $13.95
Full Magpie Dodge / Neff / $13.95
Honeymoon in Berlin / Walmsley / $16
Intensive Care / Twigg / $14
Ivanhoe Station / Neff / $10.95
Lonesome Monsters / Osborn / $10.95
Rattlesnake Plantain / Greco / $14
Sideways / Haley / $14
Singer, An Elegy / Fetherling / $14
Siren Tattoo / Greco, Mori, McIntyre / $10.95
Snatch / MacInnes / $12.95
Swing in the Hollow / Knighton / $13.95
Under the Abdominal Wall / McCartney / $11.95
Unravel / Armstrong / $16
Viral Suite / Rowley / $16
Where Words Like Monarchs Fly / McWhirter / $14.95

Write us for a free catalogue of books.

ANVIL PRESS PUBLISHERS
PO BOX 3008, MPO
VANCOUVER, BC
V6B 3X5
WWW.ANVILPRESS.COM